Take A Stand Against Bullying

VERBAL BULLYING

Jennifer Rivkin

Crabtree Publishing Company
www.crabtreebooks.com

Author: Jennifer Rivkin

Publishing plan research and development:
Sean Charlebois, Reagan Miller
Crabtree Publishing Company

Project coordinator: Kathy Middleton

Editorial director: Melissa McClellan

Art director: Tibor Choleva

Fictional Introductions: Jennifer Rivkin

Editors: Rachel Stuckey, Molly Aloian

Proofreader: Kelly McNiven

Production coordinator: Margaret Amy Salter

Prepress technician: Margaret Amy Salter

Print coordinator: Katherine Berti

Developed and produced by: BlueApple*Works* Inc.

Consultants:
Adina Herbert, MSW, RSW
Social Worker, Youth Addictions and Concurrent Disorders Service
Centre for Addiction and Mental Health, Toronto, ON, Canada

Lesley Cunningham MSW, RSW
Social Worker - Violence Prevention

Photographs: Front cover: Shutterstock; Title page: ©Mandy Godbehear/ Shutterstock Inc.; Contents page: © Jochen Schoenfeld/ Shutterstock Inc.; p. 4: ©photomak/ Shutterstock Inc.; p. 6: ©wavebreakmedia/ Shutterstock Inc.; p. 7: ©Andrey Shadrin/ Shutterstock Inc.; p. 8: ©Pixel Memoirs/ Shutterstock Inc.; p. 9 ©Junial Enterprises/ Shutterstock Inc.; p. 10 ©Lisa S./ Shutterstock Inc.; p. 11 © Mikael Damkier/ Shutterstock Inc.; p. 12 ©jamiehooper/ Shutterstock Inc.; p. 14 ©Anita Patterson Peppers/ Shutterstock Inc.; p. 15 ©Mikael Damkier/ Shutterstock Inc.; p. 16 ©Creatista/ Shutterstock Inc.; p. 18 ©Jose AS Reyes/ Shutterstock Inc.; p. 19 ©Andrey_Kuzmin/ Shutterstock Inc.; p. 20 ©enciktat/Shutterstock Inc.; p. 21 ©andrea michele piacquadio/ Shutterstock Inc.; p. 23 ©RimDream/ Shutterstock Inc.; p. 24 ©Dragon Images/ Shutterstock Inc.; p. 25 ©O Driscoll Imaging/ Shutterstock Inc.; p. 28 ©Yuri Arcurs/ Shutterstock Inc.; p. 30 ©Damir Huskic/ Shutterstock Inc.; p. 31, 34 ©Pressmaster/ Shutterstock Inc.; p. 32 © WilleeCole/ Shutterstock Inc.; p. 35 © Monkey Business Images/ Shutterstock Inc.; p. 37 ©Condor 36/ Shutterstock Inc.; p. 38 © oliveromg/ Shutterstock Inc.; p. 39 ©Tracy Whiteside/ Shutterstock Inc. torn paper background © LeksusTuss; banners:© Amgun/ Shutterstock Inc.

Library and Archives Canada Cataloguing in Publication

Rivkin, Jennifer
   Verbal bullying / Jennifer Rivkin.

(Take a stand against bullying)
Includes index.
Issued also in electronic format.
ISBN 978-0-7787-7916-2 (bound).--ISBN 978-0-7787-7921-6 (pbk.)

   1. Invective--Juvenile literature. 2. Psychological abuse--Juvenile literature. 3. Bullying--Juvenile literature. I. Title. II. Series: Take a stand against bullying

P410.I58R58 2013   j302.34'3   C2013-900252-9

Library of Congress Cataloging-in-Publication Data

Rivkin, Jennifer.
  Verbal bullying / Jennifer Rivkin.
    pages cm. -- (Take a stand against bullying)
  Includes index.
  ISBN 978-0-7787-7916-2 (reinforced library binding) -- ISBN 978-0-7787-7921-6 (pbk.) -- ISBN 978-1-4271-9077-2 (electronic pdf) -- ISBN 978-1-4271-9131-1 (electronic html)
  1. Invective--Juvenile literature. 2. Verbal behavior--Juvenile literature. 3. Bullying--Prevention--Juvenile literature. I. Title.

  BF463.I58R59 2013
  302.34'3--dc23

                  2013000564

Crabtree Publishing Company

www.crabtreebooks.com   1-800-387-7650

Printed in Canada/022013/BF20130114

Published in Canada
Crabtree Publishing
616 Welland Ave.
St. Catharines, ON
L2M 5V6

Published in the United States
Crabtree Publishing
PMB 59051
350 Fifth Avenue, 59th Floor
New York, NY 10118

Published in the United Kingdom
Crabtree Publishing
Maritime House
Basin Road North, Hove
BN41 1WR

Published in Australia
Crabtree Publishing
3 Charles Street
Coburg North
VIC, 3058

CONTENTS

When Justine stepped into the cafeteria, she scanned the room for Stephanie and, as usual, headed straight for a spot at the furthest table away from her. She sat down; her heart racing and a bead of sweat dripping from her forehead. While Justine slowly unzipped her lunchbox, she braced herself for the comments that were sure to come from the popular girl who had been picking on her since the beginning of the year.

"Ooh, what does Tubs have for lunch today?" Stephanie said loudly enough for Justine and the other kids to hear. "It's probably, like, 10 burgers and 14 brownies. She's so gross. Look, she's even sweating like a pig."

Today, Stephanie was making fun of Justine's weight, but it seemed that nothing about her was ever "acceptable" in Stephanie's eyes; her hair wasn't right, she wasn't smart enough and didn't dress "cool" enough. When Justine broke out in acne, Stephanie seemed particularly elated.

Justine looked down at her turkey sandwich, apple and cucumbers. Her mom always sent her healthy food. It was after school—when Justine thought of how much Stephanie seemed to despise her—that she did most of her eating. Sometimes it made her feel better. Mostly, it made her feel even more alone.

Today, Stephanie's words were too much. Justine felt sick to her stomach. She stood up and headed for the bathroom (where she spent many of her lunch hours these days). As she walked past Stephanie to get out of the cafeteria, Justine heard the awful "oinking" noises aimed her way. It took every ounce of her strength to hold back her tears until she had locked herself in the last stall. Once she was there, she thought that the tears would never stop.

4

INTRODUCTION
The Nature of Bullying

What Justine is experiencing is not a simple argument. Justine is a **target**. She can't get Stephanie to back off and she feels helpless. Justine is being bullied. **Bullying** is intentional, repeated, aggressive behavior intended to hurt, scare, or humiliate the victim and gain power over him or her. There are four main types of bullying: verbal bullying, **physical bullying**, **social bullying**, and **cyber bullying**. The type of bullying in Justine's case is verbal bullying, her tormentor is using words as a weapon.

In this book, you will learn what verbal bullying is, how it can hurt everyone involved, and what to do if you are being bullied or if you **witness** someone who is. You will see that it is everyone's responsibility to combat bullying. You will also discover useful strategies and tips to stop bullying after it's happened or even before it starts.

TAKE A STAND AGAINST
STOP
BULLYING

"I am very shy and quiet at school. Kids bully me on the bus and at lunch. For some reason, people don't seem to like me and they don't even know the real me! It seems like my entire grade is against me." Emma, age 13

CHAPTER 1
What is Verbal Bullying?

Verbal bullying occurs when someone uses language to hurt or gain power over another person. This includes insults, threats, name-calling, mocking, teasing, put downs, and taunts. A bully may make fun of a person's appearance and constantly call him or her "ugly," for example.

But verbal bullies aren't limited to criticizing targets for their looks. Unfortunately, there are a wide variety of things that they can choose from, such as the way people dress or play sports, gender, race, religion, ability, or sexuality. Bullies may label their victims with names such as loser, freak, or slut (and many, many, more!). With this type of bullying, the target is often tormented repeatedly over time.

How Common Is It?

If you have been bullied or witnessed someone else who has, you are not alone. In fact, one out of every four children reports being bullied—this means that millions of children are bullied each year.

Studies show that by the time you graduate from high school, each of you will have been exposed to bullying, either directly or as a witness. It is likely that you have—or will—come across verbal bullying because it is the most common type of bullying in schools. As you get older, the likelihood of physical bullying decreases, but the number of kids who use verbal, social, and cyber bullying increases. That's why it's so important to learn what you can do about it!

Who Is Involved?

There are four types of people who can be involved in verbal bullying situations:

Bully: The person who commits the verbal assault.

Target: The person on the receiving end of the verbal attack.

Bystander(s): A person or group who witnesses the bullying.

Ally(ies): A person or group who steps in to help the victim.

Most people have played each of these roles at some point.

Where Can Verbal Bullying Happen?

Not all bullying takes place at school. A bully can be in your neighborhood, on a sports team, at an extra-curricular activity, at camp—even in your own home.

While a certain amount of rivalry and arguing can be an accepted (and expected) part of a sibling relationship, sometimes, brothers or sisters can take things too far. If one sibling has power over the other and is constantly **belittling**, name-calling, or threatening the other, that is bullying. If this happens to you, you should talk to your parents about your feelings. Tell them how much it is affecting you and discuss how they can stop it by creating consequences for bullying behavior.

If the adults in your house call you nasty, hurtful names, they are being verbal bullies. Tell another adult you can trust or use one of the resources in the back of this book. They will help you figure out how to stop the bullying.

"I have been a bystander. I've watched my good friend get teased and I didn't do anything because I was scared. I feel terrible."
Jackson, age 14

Try this Experiment

To get a better idea of how a bully's words can affect a victim:

Step 1. Find a nice clean sheet of paper.

Step 2. Call the paper a name and crumple it up.

Step 3. Apologize to the paper and then smooth it out. Be sure to erase all of the wrinkles so that it looks exactly like it did in step 1.

You can still see the creases, right? That's the same effect verbal bullying has on a person. Once the words are out there, the damage can't be completely undone.

Consequences of Bullying

Anyone who has been bullied knows that a bully's words can be more painful than a punch. In fact, the emotional pain caused by verbal bullying can last way longer than a bruise or a scratch. Studies showed that adults who were bullied as children had lower self-esteem and higher levels of depression than those who were not bullied.

Bullying can have a wide range of social, emotional, physical, and mental health effects on its victims. Worrying about bullying can lead to headaches, stomachaches, and problems sleeping. Being a victim of bullying is very stressful and stress can lower the body's ability to prevent and fight off infections. Those who are bullied tend to get sick more often.

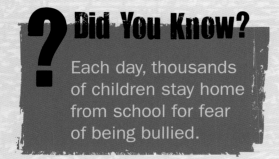

? Did You Know?

Each day, thousands of children stay home from school for fear of being bullied.

Problems in School

Verbal bullying can also lead to problems at school. If a victim is constantly worried about being verbally bullied at school, he or she may skip classes or have trouble concentrating when in class. This can lead to falling grades (which is another source of stress). The emotions that a bullying victim feels—powerlessness, loneliness, and fear—can lead to a loss of self-esteem, anxiety, and depression.

The bottom line is that bullying has serious and lasting consequences and should not be tolerated.

Sometimes, children who have been repeatedly bullied drop out of school for good. This affects them for the rest of their lives.

! Think About It!

Can you remember a time when you were a verbal bully? A victim? A **bystander**? An **ally**? What was the situation? What was said? How did you feel in each of these roles?

"I think I was born to be a magnet for bullies. They have so many things to pick on me for. They call me 'Annie' because of my red hair, 'Dot-to-dot' because of my freckles, and 'Porky' because I'm overweight. I try not to let them see me cry, but it hurts a lot. I hate looking in the mirror now because I hear their words when I look at myself." Sarah, age 14

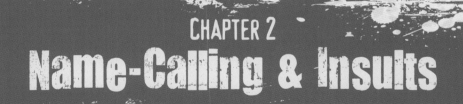

CHAPTER 2
Name-Calling & Insults

Using offensive words to exclude people, label them, humiliate them, or hurt their feelings is a form of bullying. In fact, name-calling and insults are the most frequent type of verbal bullying.

Anyone can be a victim of this type of **harassment**, but children who are visibly different in any way or who behave differently from others tend to be easy targets. They can be picked on for their race, gender, disability, or general appearance.

Verbal bullies seek out those who look different. They may make fun of kids who stand out and express themselves in unique ways with fashion or insult those who aren't wearing the latest styles and popular brands because they have chosen not to or they don't have the money to do so. Being different can be difficult, especially when everyone else seems to be trying to be alike—listening to the same music and wearing the same clothes.

Being Different

Kids who have weight issues or prominent facial features (like larger ears or noses) may be all too familiar with the awful names that can be thrown around. It probably won't take you more than a few seconds to think of five mean words to describe someone who is overweight—that's a sign of how prevalent verbal bullying is.

Too Many to List

It's impossible to come up with a full list of typical bully victims or the names that they are called. For bullies, any point of difference is fair game. Kids who need extra help with school may be called "retarded," while those who get top grades may be called out as "teacher's pets." Bullies may insult the way a person talks, their religious beliefs, disabilities, sexual identity, or physical characteristics.

"I stutter. It gets worse when I'm nervous. The teacher won't let the kids laugh at me in class, but when we're outside they imitate me and say things like 1-1-1-1-1-loser. I feel like never opening my mouth again."
Julia, age 12

Destroying One's Self-Esteem

A verbal bully's insults are always personal attacks that are intended to be extremely hurtful. The bully will come up with insults about something the victim is already sensitive about. Victims feel badly about who they are and question whether they are good enough. Each time an insult is hurled, it takes a toll on the victim's self-esteem. No matter how strong a person is to begin with, continued verbal abuse—without intervention—will have an effect that can't be shaken off. Think of verbal assaults as waves in the ocean. With time, their constant thrashing turns even the toughest rock to sand.

The R-Word

You may hear people using the word "retard," either as a harmless joke between friends or to intentionally hurt someone. In either case, it is not okay. The word is offensive and **demeans** people with intellectual disabilities. Consider joining the Spread the Word to End the Word campaign. With joining you pledge to support the elimination of the **derogatory** use of the R-word from everyday speech and promote the acceptance and inclusion of people with intellectual disabilities.

❗ Think About It!

Who gets called names in your school? What do they have in common? Has anyone called you names? How did that make you feel? Have you called anyone else names? Why did you do it and how did it make you feel about yourself?

"I'm gay. Kids at school always call me "fag." They started doing it even before I knew I was gay. Even my parents make fun of me for not being more manly. I have nowhere to go to get away from the bullying. I get called names at school and at home." Justin, age 15

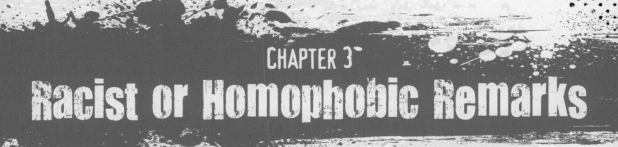

CHAPTER 3

Racist or Homophobic Remarks

Often, there are underlying **prejudices** and **stereotypes** that lead to verbal bullying. Negative thinking about race, religion, and sexuality can play a major role.

Racist stereotypes have led to a lot of suffering and harsh treatments throughout history, including ethnic oppression, slavery, and even **genocide**. Racist bullying may not be as extreme, but it is based on the same principle—treating people as inferior based on their race or color. This includes making racist jokes, **racial slurs**, mimicking a person's accent, and making negative comments about someone's race. There are stereotypes about every race and ethnicity.

Bullying based on criticizing a person's religion—including their religious dress, philosophies, and beliefs—is not uncommon and is equally as hurtful.

Sexual Orientation

Discrimination based on **sexual orientation,** or assumed sexual orientation, is a factor in another form of verbal bullying—**homophobic** remarks. How often have you heard a person at school refer to something or someone as "gay"?

The words "gay" and "fag" have become more and more common attack words used by bullies. They are damaging on many levels. If a victim does identify as lesbian, gay, bisexual or **transgendered** (LGBT), feeling unaccepted can make them question their self-worth.

Even Your Hobbies!

Others may be targeted because they don't conform to **gender stereotypes**. Perhaps they are judged as acting "too masculine" or "too feminine." Girls who play basketball or dress in less-feminine clothing may be called "dyke," while boys who like ballet or drama may be called "gay." This is also destructive for the victim's self-esteem.

Feeling unaccepted can lead to isolation and severe depression.

People should be able to express themselves in any way they choose, and should not be forced into strict gender roles to fit in.

Did You Know?

Another study found that 64 percent of LGBT students feel unsafe at school.

It's the Bully Who is Wrong

Anti-gay bullying affects everyone. Some victims are harassed with anti-gay slurs for no reason except that the bully wants to hurt them. If someone is insulting and bullying you, try to remember one thing: there is no reason for you to be picked on and no one deserves to be insulted or bullied. It's the bully who is behaving badly, not you.

What's wrong is the bullying, not you or anything about you.

Everyone has the right to feel safe and be treated respectfully regardless of their sexual orientation, race, or religion.

"I am a Muslim and I am proud of it. I am not violent. The Quran, which is the holy book of Islam, teaches peace and kindness. What the terrorists do is the opposite of what the Quran says, but the people at school don't understand that. They call me names like Bin Laden. I just want to express my faith and not have to hide who I am."

Maryam, age 15

Race and Religion

While racist or religious slurs do not physically harm individuals, they can damage self-esteem and make people question the value of their differences. They are particularly hurtful because they disparage a person's history, belief system, and culture, which is a huge part of who they are.

"I have absolutely no friends at my school. Everyone is always picking on me because I'm Jewish and both my parents are doctors. I get good grades, and they say that I'm the typical Jew that will become a doctor, lawyer, or accountant. They are always making Jew jokes, especially when we're learning about the Holocaust...I dread going to school every day." Josh, age 13

! Think About It!

Make a list of some personal characteristics or activities that you associate with being masculine or feminine. Why do you associate these with one or the other gender? How can this be harmful? Why do you think that the term "gay" has become such a common put down? What can you do to make a change?

"Last year, a boy from another class decided to pick on me because of my weight. Every time I walked by him he snorted like a pig. His friends all laughed. I'd get so scared when I had to leave my classroom. I didn't want to be in the halls, the lunchroom, or outside. Some days I couldn't even deal with it, so I faked sick. I cried every day after school." Gemma, age 12

CHAPTER 4
Understanding the Victim

Anyone can be a target of a verbal taunt once in a while, but taunting doesn't always lead to a repeated pattern of bullying. There are some characteristics that can make it more likely for a person to become a victim of verbal bullying over time.

Many victims of verbal bullying are shyer and less assertive than their peers. They can be described as passive victims in that they don't provoke their bully, nor do they defend themselves or report the incident. Instead, they may cry or back away. Unfortunately, this may boost a bully's feeling of power, which is what he or she is seeking. Bullies don't generally choose victims who are likely to retaliate; they choose people that they think will be easy targets.

? Did You Know?

It is a myth that bullying will go away when it's ignored by all.

Who Makes an "Easy Target"?

There is no exact formula for determining who might be a victim of verbal bullying, but these factors can make it more likely:

- Being new at the school
- Being small or young
- Being sensitive (e.g. crying when confronted) or anxious
- Having low self-confidence
- Being shy
- Engaging in behaviors that others find irritating
- Having few friends

"I was bullied at school for years. The kids were awful. They called me fat and ugly. I tried getting help, but it didn't work. The teachers and school counselor told me to ignore them. That did nothing. Finally, my friends stepped in and told the teachers. I think it took that for the teachers to realize how serious it was. They talked to the bullies. It's gotten better. Don't give up. It will work eventually."
David, age 14

Not the Victim's Fault

While there are certainly some traits that can make a person more likely to be a target of verbal bullying, it is never the victim's fault. A verbal bully can choose anything about a person to pick on, so changing the way you are to suit the bully isn't the answer—it gives them the power they are looking for and it undervalues your individuality.

In addition to the factors on the previous page, other things such as race, perceived sexual orientation, religious beliefs, national origin, perceived intelligence (either gifted or special needs), disability, or appearance (being short, tall, overweight, skinny, dressing differently) can make you more likely to be a target. You'll notice that this list covers the majority of people!

It's not your uniqueness that must change; it's the culture around bullying. So what can you do? The first step is telling someone.

Is It Okay to Tell?

It is more than okay—it is the right thing to do. Reporting bullies can stop them from hurting you and others. You may fear that people will say you are "ratting someone out" if you tell. Words like "tattle," "snitch," or "rat" have negative connotations and are used to intimidate people into silence. If you are reporting a bully, you are not trying to get someone in trouble. You are stopping a bully from doing any more harm and helping to keep everyone safe.

If someone verbally attacks you or a friend once, you can wait and see what happens. If it happens more than once, it's time to tell. The longer it goes on, the more it will become a cycle and the harder it will be to stop.

Talk openly and honestly with your parents about the bullying. If it is occurring at school, tell a teacher, counselor, or principal. If you are afraid of retaliation, you can remain **anonymous**. Go when the bully is not around. Take a friend with you—there is strength in numbers. Or, write an anonymous note to the teacher or principal explaining what has happened.

? Did You Know?

Many students feel that adult intervention won't help and they fear that telling adults will only bring more harassment from bullies.

Remember: Verbal bullying is not something you just have to live with or ignore, it is not a regular and acceptable part of growing up.

Creating a Target

Some natural personality traits can be like bait for bullies, but it can also work the other way around. That is, a target may be selected randomly and the victim's personality changes as a result of bullying. Kids who were once happy and outgoing can become depressed and mistrustful. If they start believing the bad things said about them, they may become shy and nervous, landing them in the easy target category for bullies.

"I was bullied when I was little. I had no friends and I hated school. When I finally made friends, I was so happy. But for some reason, I would make fun of them and make them feel bad about themselves. Basically, I bullied them. I lost those friends, but I'm trying to learn from that and be a better friend in the future. I don't want it to happen again." Taryn, age 12

Think About It!

Why do you think that targets of bullying do not always escape the cycle when they move to a different school? Why do bullies often choose kids who are "different" to pick on? Do you think this type of intolerance happens with adults, too? What can be done about it?

"I admit it. I'm a bully. It's not that I beat people up or anything, but I say things to hurt them. I'm small and people used to call me names. One day, I realized that even though I couldn't physically hurt them, my words could do damage. I felt powerful when I made kids cry. I still verbally bully people if they annoy me. I try to break them down. It's who I am." Trevor, age 13

 Understanding the Bully

So, now that you know the consequences of bullying, you may be wondering why someone would set out to deliberately hurt another person with words. Just like their victims, bullies come in all shapes and sizes and from all backgrounds.

There is a myth that all bullies are angry, have problems at home, and problems adjusting at school. It's true that some children who bully come from homes with conflict—they may watch a parent being bullied, or be bullied directly by their parents or siblings. Some bullies are also impulsive and have low self-esteem. This type of bully tends to be jealous, lose his or her temper quickly, and mistake others friendly actions for hostile actions. For example, a bully may think someone is disrespecting them when they are actually making an innocent comment or suggestion. These bullies also lack **empathy** for others. But new research shows that less than half of kids who bully fit this profile.

Don't Bully Yourself

Have you ever called yourself names in your head? Telling yourself that you are fat, stupid, or ugly is like bullying yourself (and you can never escape this particular bully). Try to be aware of what you say to yourself and treat yourself as kindly as you should treat other people.

Only the "Big, Bad Bully"?

You may be surprised to find out that bullies have high self-esteem and good social skills, are popular, do well in school, get along with adults, and are generally happy. While you may have read about the "big, bad bully" in books or seen them on TV, in real life, anyone is capable of being a bully. We have all said things that are unkind. Some people who are considered bullies may not even be aware that others view them that way.

? Did You Know?

Children who observe bullying that goes unchecked or is ignored by adults are at greater risk of becoming bullies themselves. One out of every five kids admits to bullying.

Seeking Power

Bullies are not all alike in their characters, but their motivations are the same—they are seeking power over others. Some do this because they believe it will protect them from being bullied themselves, they have been bullied in the past, or they have low self-esteem and are attempting to feel better by demeaning others. But more use verbal aggression as a way to achieve and maintain the popularity that they feel they are entitled to. Let's face it, being powerful and having status in the peer group feels good.

Sometimes people bully in groups. As a group, they are looking to establish dominance. Individuals take part in the name calling to fit in and be popular with their peers.

? Did You Know?

Boys tend to bully according to group, such as athlete versus non-athlete. Girls tend to bully according to social status, such as popular versus unpopular.

Boys or Girls?

While boys and girls can both be bullies, boys who bully tend to use physical or verbal bullying. Boys use their size and strength to intimidate, while girls use more social forms like gossip and exclusion in order to maintain popularity. However, over the last several decades, the difference between boys and girls may be getting less pronounced, with girls becoming more violent and boys engaging in more social bullying—not the type of gender equality we are striving for!

Bullying Hurts...Everyone

Did you know that bullies also harm themselves when they verbally abuse others?

By targeting others, bullies learn and reinforce negative social interactions. They don't learn social skills like sharing and empathy. Making people scared of you and making others feel badly doesn't build real friendships or respect. Most bullies eventually lose friends. After all, who wants to be friends with someone who is mean?

If the behavior is left unchecked, bullies can become adults with anti-social behavior, drug and alcohol addiction, depression, and even an increased risk of suicide. One study found that 60 percent of boys who bully others in elementary school had criminal records by age 24. Even if it doesn't reach this extreme, continuing with this behavior past school can lead to problems at work and with relationships.

It could also get you into some real trouble. These days, bullying is taken more seriously than ever before. Under the law it can result in suspension, expulsion, or criminal action that can affect your future.

Think About It!

Have you ever used your words to hurt someone? Why did you do it? How did you feel afterward? Do you know someone who is a verbal bully? What are they like? How do you think this behavior is affecting them? What do you think will happen if they continue?

"In the past, I've been a bully, I've been a victim and I've been the bystander. Now, I stand up for myself and for anyone I see who is getting bullied. I know what it feels like and I don't want anyone else to go through it. I tell the bullies that they are being ridiculous. Sometimes it works." Joaquín, age 14

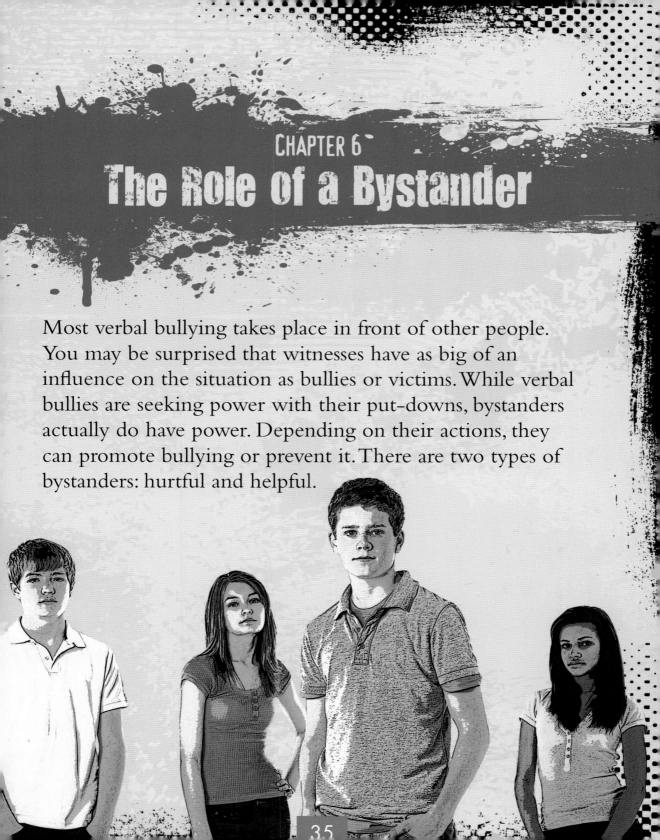

CHAPTER 6
The Role of a Bystander

Most verbal bullying takes place in front of other people. You may be surprised that witnesses have as big of an influence on the situation as bullies or victims. While verbal bullies are seeking power with their put-downs, bystanders actually do have power. Depending on their actions, they can promote bullying or prevent it. There are two types of bystanders: hurtful and helpful.

"When I started my new school, I worried that I wasn't going to have any friends. I tried to get in with the cool kids. I did whatever it took to fit in. I called people names like "loser" and treated kids that weren't popular like garbage. It worked. I was really popular. Then I started losing my friends one by one. It took being alone for me to realize that what I did was wrong."
Jessie, age 16

Hurtful Bystanders

Some bystanders join forces with the bully and egg them on, either by laughing or by adding to the insults that are being thrown at the victim. Bystanders might act this way because they have little empathy for the victim, they feel that he or she deserves it, they are friends with the bully, or they are bullies themselves. Others may not be as eager to join in, but take part because they want to be popular and get on the bully's good side—or stay off of his or her bad side.

But it's not just kids that open their mouths in support of the bully who do damage—those that keep their mouths shut hurt the victim as well. These bystanders are an audience for the bully, who may get a kick out of being in the spotlight.

They don't directly encourage the bully, but they help him or her get away with it by remaining silent. When a bully sees that no one steps in, he or she has no reason to stop, and may even think that the bystanders agree with the taunts. Watching bullying and doing nothing is, in effect, saying it's okay. What makes it even worse is that when the victim feels ganged up on the negative consequences of bullying are magnified. By doing nothing, the bystander also becomes a bully.

Helpful Bystanders

Helpful bystanders to bullying are also called "allies." Allies are those who step up to help the victim. They can (ideally) intervene while the incident is happening by telling the bully to stop and encouraging other bystanders to do the same. Or, they can go get an adult who can help or report the incident afterwards.

"I have seen kids being called names, and I admit that I have been a bystander. Watching it happen, and not doing anything, made me feel weak." Alexis, age 16

Why Don't More Bystanders Intervene?

When bystanders don't step in, they often feel guilty, weak, and anxious afterward. Still, many remain silent because stepping in can be scary. Bystanders worry about retribution from the bully—they don't want to become the target themselves or they fear they will slip in popularity or be labeled a "rat."

Witnesses may also stand back because they don't know how to help or they don't realize the impact they can have on the situation. They may think, "There's nothing I can do," or "It's not my business." If you've read this far, you know better. You know that bullying is everyone's problem and that you can do something to stop it.

Bystanders often feel guilty if they do not help a victim of bullying.

What to Do if You Witness Verbal Bullying

Think about how you would feel if you were the one at the receiving end of the verbal bullying. You would want someone in your corner, right? You can be that person.

It can be as simple as telling the bully to stop. Don't sink to the bully's level by calling him or her names. A simple "Don't say that. It's not funny," or "That's not cool" will do. Ask your fellow bystanders to help. You can also ask the target to walk away from the situation with you. Tell him or her that what happened is not okay and that the incident should be reported. If you don't feel safe speaking up in the moment or leaving with the victim, it's okay. Walk away and report the incident to a teacher in person or by writing a note.

When you see somebody being bullied, step in and help the victim. It will boost your self-confidence.

Think About It!

Have you ever seen someone being bullied? What did you do? What would you do now?

CHAPTER 7

Empowering Yourself:
What You Can Do if You Are Being Bullied

Well-meaning people may have told you to just ignore bullying. Unfortunately, that doesn't always work. What does help is getting help. You don't need to face it alone.

? Did You Know?

Bullying isn't good for anyone—not the victim, bystander, or bully. If bullying isn't stopped, it can become a chronic cycle that can last for years.

You can ask for help at school from teachers, counselors, or the principal. Many schools already have prevention programs in place. Under new legislation, it is your school's responsibility to provide a safe environment for learning. You can ask for help at home. Talk to your parents or siblings—aunts, uncles, and grandparents are usually happy to lend an ear, too. There are also many resources in your community, including websites and helplines that are set up to help you deal with what you are going through.

Work on building alliances with kids at school. Try to find someone to be with at lunch, recess, and walking home. Join all the extra-curricular activities you can to meet more kids. Take steps to build your own self-confidence.

Tips for Standing Up to Bullies

Be Assertive with Your Body Language: If you are slouching or have your head down, a bully may feel that you are an easy target. Stand up straight, keep your head high, and make eye contact with the bully.

Speak Up: Speak confidently and firmly and tell the bully that you will not be a victim. Use your own words to say something to the effect of "back off." Do what you can to send the message that you won't put up with it. Practice this at home or role-play with a friend, so that when the time comes, you are ready.

Don't Stoop to Their Level: Do not call bullies names or threaten them.

Report the Bullying: If you are being called names or teased, speak up. As you learned earlier, "reporting" is not "ratting."

Become an Ally: If you have a friend who is bullying, talk privately to them and tell them that you think they should stop and why. If you have a friend or peer who is bullied, stand up for him or her—just like you would want someone to do for you.

Start a Program: If you don't have an anti-bullying program or group in your school, talk to your principal about starting one.

Don't Give Up: You may have tried to get help before. If it didn't work, keep trying to have your voice heard. It may take some time, and you may have to try a few different tactics, but it can get better. The most important thing to remember is that you are worth fighting for. If it ever feels hopeless, it can help to look toward the future. Make a list of things that you are looking forward to.

Bullying: Then and Now

Bullying is not a new phenomenon. Just ask your parents, grandparents, or great grandparents! Your parents may tell you about children with glasses being called "four-eyes" and your great-grandparents may tell you about pigtails being dipped in inkwells (you can look that one up later).

What is different these days are people's attitudes toward bullies. In the past, when it came to bullying, many adults would say things like "kids will be kids" or "it will toughen them up." We now know that neither of those sayings is true. Kids don't have to bully or be bullied, and being bullied doesn't necessarily make kids strong, it can also make them insecure.

A more appropriate saying for today is "when you know better, you do better." Now that we know the damaging effects of verbal bullying, we can no longer stand by and watch it happen. That's why many schools now have a zero-tolerance policy for bullying to promote a positive and safe learning environment.

Bullying in schools was just as common in the past as it is now.

Anti-bullying campaigns are also raising awareness. In 2000, anti-bullying activist Bill Belsey created the first National Bullying Prevention Week in Canada. In 2006, PACER's National Bullying Prevention Center (pacer.org) declared that October would be National Bullying Prevention month in the United States.

Campaigns like "Pink Shirt Day" (pinkshirtday.ca) and others help raise awareness, too. On Pink Shirt Day, students are encouraged to wear something pink to symbolize that bullying will not be tolerated. The idea started with David Shepherd and Travis Price, two high school seniors in Nova Scotia who organized a protest in an effort to stand up for a freshman boy who was being harassed for wearing pink. They handed out 50 pink tank tops to the boys in their school. It worked! Now, Pink Shirt Day is an annual event at many schools.

PACER invites people to wear orange on Unity Day in October. Their Make it Orange and Make it End! campaign against bullying is supported by television personalities like Anderson Cooper and Ellen DeGeneres, who wear orange to remind their viewers about the importance of standing up against bullying.

There are similar campaigns across North America, but no matter the color of the shirt, the message is the same. Bullying must stop.

Think About It!

Make a list of people that you can talk to if you need help. If someone came to you for advice, what would you say to them if they were a bully? Bystander? Target?

Are You a Verbal Bully?

You have probably hurt someone's feelings, either intentionally or unintentionally, or made comments that you regretted later. But are these unusual events, or could you be a bully? Think back on this school year and answer these questions:

1. Did I make fun of someone's appearance?
2. Did I make fun of someone's religion, race, or nationality? Even as a joke?
3. Did I try to intimidate or threaten someone to get what I want?
4. Did I call anyone names?
5. Did I curse or swear at anyone?
6. Did I say something hurtful and then say, "Just kidding?"
7. Did I try to hurt someone's feelings or put them down? Did I like the result?
8. Do I have trouble controlling my anger?
9. Is it hard for me to censor my words? Do they just seem to come out before I know it?
10. Have I witnessed verbal bullying in my own home?
11. Am I bullied at home or school?
12. Do I put others down because I want to become/remain popular?

If you answered yes to any of these questions, and it's happened more than once, you may be a bully.

If You're a Bully

If you recognize yourself as a bully, this book is as important for you as it is for victims. You may not have realized how much your bullying was hurting others—and yourself. It's not too late to stop. Bullying is a behavior and behaviors can be changed.

First, consider how you have made people feel, and make a list of reasons you should stop. Apologize to your victims, tell them it won't happen again, and mean what you say. Then, think about why you did it. Were you trying to feel better about yourself? Were you trying to be popular? These aren't excuses, but it helps to know that they are triggers for your bullying. Learn to stop it before it starts. For example, if your concern is popularity, think of positive ways to be popular. Being kind and funny can be more effective than using scare tactics.

Talk to an adult and ask them for advice on resolving conflicts. If your home life has been part of the problem, or your temper is an issue, you may consider speaking with a counselor or using a resource like Kids Help Phone or the Boys Town National Hotline. Change can be difficult at first, but it will get easier.

Other Resources

If you are dealing with bullying—either as a target, bystander, or bully—you don't have to go through it alone. There is information out there and people who are waiting to help. Don't hesitate to reach out if you need them.

Books

Dear Bully: 70 Authors Tell Their Stories, edited by Megan Kelley Hall and Carrie Jones. (HarperTeen, 2011).

Your favorite writers, including R.L. Stine, share essays about their experiences as either a victim, bully, or bystander. There are some great lessons to be learned from the experiences of people who have gone before you. You're in good company!

Bullied: What Every Parent, Teacher and Kid Needs to Know About Ending the Cycle of Fear, by Carrie Goldman (HaperOne, 2012).

This book features personal stories as well as concrete tips to end bullying. Have a read, and then pass it along to your parents and teachers. Putting an end to bullying must be a joint effort.

Websites

PrevNet: Promoting Relationships and Eliminating Violence
www.prevnet.ca

This website features useful resources and information for victims, bullies, and bystanders.

PACER National Bullying Prevention Center
www.pacer.org/bullying

This informative site has great stories, videos, and up-to-date resources to help prevent bullying. Empower yourself by joining PACER's Kids Against Bullying Organization and become part of the solution.

Pink Shirt Day
www.pinkshirtday.ca

On this site, you can learn more about how anti-bullying campaigns draw attention to the problem, and be inspired to join or start one in your area.

Organizations, Hotlines, and Helplines

Kids Help Phone (Canada) (1-800-668-6868)
www.kidshelpphone.ca

Professional counselors can answer your questions on-line or by phone with this free, confidential service. It's open 24/7, 365 days a year.

Boys Town National Hotline (United States) (1-800-448-3000)
www.yourlifeyourvoice.org

In the United States, both boys and girls can call this national hotline to talk to a counselor about anything at anytime.

My Gay Straight Alliance (Canada) (www.mygsa.ca)

MGSA.ca is Canada's website for safer and inclusive schools for the lesbian, gay, bisexual, trans, queer, and questioning (LGBTQ) community.

National Suicide Prevention Lifeline (United States) (1-800-273-TALK)
www.suicidepreventionlifeline.org

If you are having suicidal thoughts, call or chat online with a counselor now. They care and are waiting to help you.

The Trevor Project (United States) (866-4-U-TREVOR)
www.thetrevorproject.org

The Trevor Project provides crisis intervention and suicide prevention services to lesbian, gay, bisexual, transgender, and questioning youth.

Stomp Out Bullying Help Line (United States) (855-790-4357)
www.stompoutbullying.org/livechat_portal.php

This Live Help Chat Line is free and confidential for kids over 13. The counselors have been trained to help victims of bullying.

Glossary

ally A person who is on someone's side, a supporter

anonymous Not named or identified

belittling To make someone feel small or unimportant

bullying Repeated, aggressive behavior intended to hurt and to gain power over the victim

bystander A person who is present at an incident but does not take part

cyber bullying Using technology (email, texts, blogs, social networking sites) to intimidate a person, hurt their feelings, or damage their reputation

demean To lower someone's status or reputation

derogatory Expression of a low opinion of someone

discrimination The unjust or prejudicial treatment of different categories of people, especially on the grounds of race, age, or sex

empathy Understanding what another person is feeling; being able to put yourself in their shoes

gender stereotype An idea about the way men or women are "supposed" to act or dress

genocide The deliberate destruction of a large group of people, especially ones of a specific ethnic group

harassment Repeatedly attacking, upsetting, or intimidating someone

heterosexual A person who is attracted to the opposite sex

homophopia Thinking less of people who are gay or lesbian

physical bullying Hitting, punching, kicking, slapping, or any act of physical violence

prejudices An unfavorable opinion directed against an individual, a group, or a race

racial slur A disrespectful term that treats another race as lesser than your own

sexual orientation Identity based on whether a person is attracted to the same sex (gay, lesbian), the opposite sex (heterosexual), or both sexes (bisexual)

social bullying Intentionally damaging someone's social life or relationships. It can involve excluding someone from a group on purpose, spreading rumors, or telling others to avoid the target

stereotypes An assumption about the traits of a category of people

target The person selected as the aim of an attack

transgender People whose characteristics or appearance do not match the physical gender to which they were born

witness To see something happen

Index